Meet the Muppet Man

By Alan Trussell-Cullen

Dominie Press, Inc.

Publisher: Raymond Yuen
Project Editor: John S. F. Graham
Editor: Bob Rowland
Designer: Greg DiGenti
Photographs: Bettmann/Corbis (Cover, pages 9, 17, 19, and 22)

Muppets and Muppet images are trademarks of
The Jim Henson Co. & Muppets, Inc.

Published by:

ꟼ Dominie Press, Inc.

1949 Kellogg Avenue
Carlsbad, California 92008 USA

www.dominie.com

1-800-232-4570

Paperback ISBN 0-7685-1837-7
Printed in Singapore by PH Productions Pte Ltd
1 2 3 4 5 6 PH 05 04 03

Table of Contents

Chapter One

Do You Know the Muppet Man?

Just about everyone knows who Kermit
the Frog is. They know Miss Piggy and
Big Bird, too. In fact, millions of children
all over the world have come to know
and love all the Muppet characters.

This is the story about the man who

created the Muppets. His name was Jim Henson, and he was born in 1936 in the small town of Leland, Missouri.

When Jim was in high school, his family moved to Washington. He enjoyed school, but he loved watching television, too.

In 1954, he was getting ready to go to college. He heard that a local TV station needed someone to do some work with puppets on a children's show over the summer months. Jim didn't know much about puppets, but he really wanted to get on TV. He and a friend made a couple of puppets. They took them to the TV station and were given a job.

The job didn't last long, but Jim's life would never be the same again. He had fallen in love with puppets.

A few months later, he started working with puppets on another TV station. It wasn't long before they let him have his own five-minute program. It was called "Sam and Friends." The show was broadcast twice a day and ran for six years. At the same time, Jim continued working his way through college. One of the students who came to help him on "Sam and Friends" was Jane Nebel. Jane and Jim were married in 1959.

One day, Jim wanted to make a new puppet for "Sam and Friends." He needed some cloth, so he used an old green coat that his mother no longer wanted. So, what kind of creature do you make out of green cloth? That's how Kermit the Frog began.

Jim loved all his puppets, but Kermit quickly became his favorite. Jim had many helpers to work his other puppets, but he always insisted on working Kermit himself.

While doing "Sam and Friends," Jim thought a lot about what kind of puppets worked well on TV. In those days, hand puppets usually had faces that were made out of wood, so they kept the same facial expression. But Jim wanted puppets that had life and showed their feelings. So he made cloth puppets that had soft faces. This meant the puppeteer's hand inside the head could make the puppet change its facial expression. Kermit can smile, frown, look puzzled, look happy, even laugh—just like a person.

Learning to be a good Muppeteer takes a long time and plenty of practice. This is because a Muppet is really two kinds of puppet in one—a *glove* puppet and a *rod* puppet, a kind of marionette.

Jim Henson with Kermit (top) and Ernie

With a glove puppet, the puppeteer's hands work the puppet from inside—the fingers move the head and the arms. With a rod puppet, the puppet is held up from below on sticks, and the arms are moved from below by rods or wires.

With Kermit and his other characters, Jim had invented a new kind of puppet, so he needed a new name for it. It wasn't quite a marionette, and it wasn't an ordinary puppet, either. So he made up a new name for his kind of puppets— *Muppets*.

Chapter Two

The Muppets on "Sesame Street"

Throughout the early 1960s, the Muppet family continued to grow. The Muppets made many appearances on a range of TV shows, including "The Today Show" and "The Ed Sullivan Show." But Jim's next big break came in 1969, when he was invited to provide the puppets on a new children's program that was being prepared by the Children's Television Workshop. The program was "Sesame Street."

The program was for three- to four-year-olds to help prepare them for school. The Children's Television Workshop wanted puppets that would be able to reflect the way children that age feel about themselves and their world.

Jim and his team of Muppeteers got to work. They created a whole range of wonderful characters for the show, including Big Bird, Bert and Ernie, the Cookie Monster, the Count, and Oscar the Grouch. Some old favorites, like Kermit the Frog, also appeared.

"Sesame Street" was an instant success. The program was soon being broadcast daily to more than six million children in the United States, and it was also being watched by millions of children in other countries around the world. An important part of that success was due to Jim Henson's Muppets.

Chapter Three
"The Muppet Show"

"**S**esame Street" brought the Muppets to a much wider audience. But Jim Henson wanted to be more than a children's entertainer. He believed his Muppets could entertain people of all ages. He approached the big TV networks to try to get them interested in producing a TV series for family viewing. Unfortunately, the networks were not very interested.

But over in England, a TV producer named Lord Lew Grade had other ideas. He had seen the Muppets, and he was hooked. He invited Jim to come to London to produce "The Muppet Show" there. The show could then be shown in England and also to U.S. audiences through stations that were not part of the big networks. Jim's dream of having a Muppet show for all ages in prime-time TV was about to happen.

Much work had to be done. Scripts had to be written. New Muppets had to be made. Sets had to be designed and built. Special "Muppet Show" music had to be written and rehearsed. Hundreds of people were soon hard at work. And to make matters even more complicated, while "The Muppet Show" was being produced and recorded in London, many in the Muppet team were still back in New York, making "Sesame Street." Going to work on "The Muppet Show" often meant having to get on a plane and fly across the Atlantic Ocean!

Jim and his writers decided that "The Muppet Show" would be about a group of Muppets who are putting on their own live show.

A number of new characters were created for "The Muppet Show," like Statler and Waldorf, the two critics who sit in their theater box and heckle the stars.

One famous character created for "The Muppet Show" happened by accident. The script for "The Muppet

Kermit and Miss Piggy on "The Muppet Show"

Show" pilot called for Kermit to appear with a chorus of barnyard animals all singing together. There were cows, chickens, and pigs.

One of the fun things about working on "The Muppet Show" was that people didn't always follow the script. They

17

loved to kid around and make up things as they went along. (Actors call this ad-libbing.) When one of the pigs was supposed to sing a solo, Frank Oz, who was operating the pig, decided to have a little fun. Instead of staying in the chorus line, he made her come down and start flirting with Kermit. Everyone said, "Wow! That pig has attitude! She has to stay!" And so, overnight, Miss Piggy became a star!

It's a chaotic business for the Muppets backstage on their "set." Everything that can go wrong usually does. But Kermit is there to try to hold the show together and keep it going.

For each show, there is a human guest who sings and dances with some of the Muppets. People who have appeared on "The Muppet Show" include Billy

Singer Linda Ronstadt performs on "The Muppet Show" with some Muppet musicians. A Muppeteer is in the background, operating both the trumpet player and Elmo, who is singing along.

Crystal, Sylvester Stallone, Brooke Shields, Steve Martin, and Sandra Bullock.

Chapter Four

The Muppets Go to Hollywood

"The Muppet Show" was an amazing success. By the end of its third season, it had been watched by more than 235 million people in more than 100 countries! By now, Jim and his crew were thinking of doing a movie with the Muppets.

The first Muppet movie opened in the United States in 1979 and was a huge success. Many of the Muppets became stars in their own right. Kermit got to host "The Tonight Show" in 1979, and Miss Piggy and Kermit appeared on the cover of *Life* magazine.

The movie was so successful that Jim Henson decided to bring the TV "Muppet Show" to an end and concentrate on making movies. Two more Muppet movies followed—*The Great Muppet Caper* and *The Muppets Take Manhattan.*

Jim Henson had truly followed his dream. His Muppets were known and loved all around the world. But he had many projects he wanted to do, and he continued to push himself.

He flew around the United States and all over the world just to oversee all the

Jim Henson with many of his Muppet creations

exciting things his company was doing.

On May 4, 1990, he made a guest appearance on a TV show in Los Angeles. After the show, he said he felt a little tired and had a sore throat. But he didn't think any more about it, and flew back to New York.

The next weekend he flew to North Carolina with his daughter to visit his father and stepmother. He still had the sore throat and was still feeling tired, but it was restful being with his family and friends.

On Sunday, he flew back to New York. He was supposed to be working on a Muppet recording session, but he cancelled it. His friends were now starting to worry. Jim was rarely sick! By four in the morning on Tuesday, Jim knew he was very ill. He was rushed to a hospital with a very serious form of pneumonia. The doctors did all they could, but he died the following morning. He was 54.

A memorial service was held for Jim on May 21, 1990. Five thousand people came, all dressed in bright colors, as Jim had requested, and all intent on celebrating his wonderful life. Jim's fellow Muppeteers had made 2,000 foam butterflies on rods, and these fluttered in the air throughout the ceremony. Hanging over the entrance to the church was an old green coat, missing a frog-shaped piece of cloth. It was a celebration of his life.

In his life, Jim Henson brought laughter and happiness to millions of children and their families around the world.